THE ALPHABET CONSPIRACY

THE ALPHABET CONSPIRACY

POEMS

Rita Mae Reese

ARKTOI BOOKS | PASADENA, CALIFORNIA

The Alphabet Conspiracy

Book design by Mark E. Cull
Book layout by Leila Benoun

Library of Congress Cataloging-in-Publication Data
Reese, Rita Mae.
The alphabet conspiracy : poems / Rita Mae Reese.—1st ed.
    p. cm.
ISBN 978-0-9800407-3-9
I. Title.
PS3618.E4423A79 2011
811'.6—dc22
                              2010042321

Arktoi Books is an imprint of Red Hen Press
First Edition

ACKNOWLEDGMENTS

Grateful acknowledgment is given to the following publications in which poems from this collection first appeared, sometimes in altered versions: "Almanac" and "Ur: What Signs & Wonders" in *32 Poems*; "Intercession" (as "There are no patron saints against accidents") and "Smite, Smitten" in *Anti-Poetry*; "Meaning *To Milk*," "Mishap," "*The Whore's Guide to Etymology*," and "Within Five Miles of Home" in *Blackbird*; "The Plagiarist" and "This Is Not True" in *Bloom*; "Dear Reader" in *Broken Bridge Review*; "Spurious Entry" in *Cimarron Review*; "The Opposite of Falling Stars, 1978" and "Monongah, 1907" in *Connotation Press: An Online Artifact*; "For Western Violence and Brief Sensuality: A Rondeau" in *Cream City Review*; "Seed Store Sestina" in *Kestrel*; "You Bring Out the Dead in Me" in *Memorious*; "The American On His First Honeymoon" in *Mid-American Review*; "Lilith vs. the Movie Monsters" (as "The Alchemist's Daughter Learns to Masturbate") and "Whatever You Do" (as "The Zookeeper's Daughter Drives to the Store") in *Mississippi Review Online*; "A History of Glass" in *The Nation*; "Who Will Give My Father a Needle, a Mouse, a Cat, a Bird?" and "In the ER Waiting Room with My Girlfriend" in *The Normal School*; "The Sin-Eater" in *The Pinch*; "My Mother Crochets the Lord's Last Supper" in *River Styx*; "*Terrible Holy Joy:* Reading the Norton Anthology of Poetry in Bed" in *The Rondeau Roundup*; "On the Maiden Voyage of Francis Marion, Revolutionary War Hero," "Staying Under" and "Civic Duty" in *Sand Hill Review*; "Bondmaid," "Key to Pronunciation: /sälm/" and "Womanless" in *The Southern Review*; "Auto Life Fire" in *Switched-on Gutenberg*; "The Alphabet Conspiracy" in *Sycamore Review*; "This is the final day of sweetness" in *Tupelo Press Poetry Projec*t; "Key to Pronunciation: /sälm/" in *Verse Daily*. "Saint Rita" and "My Mother Crochets the Lord's Last Supper" also appear in *Wild Sweet Notes II: More West Virginia Poetry*. "Seed Store Sestina" also appears in *The Artist as Activist in Appalachia*.

I would like to thank the following for helping make this book possible:

Eloise Klein Healy for her vision and support and Nickole Brown for bringing everything together so beautifully; the Program in Creative Writing at the University of Wisconsin-Madison for awarding me the Martha Meier Renk Distinguished Graduate Fellowship in Poetry; the Rona Jaffe Foundation and the Stegner fellowship for their generosity and encouragement; my students who make it a joy; all of my friends and teachers, including Cathy Attig and the wonderful people at the *Dictionary of American Regional English*, Stacy Brand, Lisa Marie Brodsky, Janet Burroway, Robert Olen Butler, David Camphouse, Heather Dubrow, Keith Ekiss, Kimberly Elkins, Kevin A. González, Emily Green, Michael Haines, Frances Hartnett, Hunt Hawkins, Maria Hummel, Jesse Lee Kercheval, David Kirby, Nick Lantz, Sandra Marshburn, Sara Michas-Martin, Roen Montalva, Lorrie Moore, Elise Paschen, Preston Richardson, Suzanne Rivecca, Kristen Rouse (my first and always toughest editor), Elizabeth Stuckey-French, Alexandra Teague, Lu Vickers, and Ron Wallace.

A special thanks to Barbara Hamby, who started it all; Denise Miller who unlocked the words; and Brandy T. Wilson, who made it fun (and when it couldn't be fun made it bearable).

And to Elizabeth, who makes everything possible.

for my family

Contents

Plots, true or false, are necessary things.
  —John Dryden
    from "Absalom and Achitophel"

INTERCESSION

There are patron saints for archives and Arkansas and advertisers.
Against dying alone.

For backward children, boxers and boys' choirs.
For birds and breastfeeding.

For cancer patients, pastry chefs and good confessions.
For country girls and criminals.
Against cold.

For dancers, the recently dead and dentists.
Against sudden death.

For engineers, exiles and evil spirits.
Against eating disorders and enemy plots.
Against earaches and earthquakes.

For fathers and fugitives and forgotten causes and Florida.
Against frenzy.

For gas station workers and guards and the Greek Air Force.
Against gout.

For hostages, hangovers and hardware stores.
Against sick horses and hair loss. Against hesitation.

For inquisitors, ice skating and the cooks of Italy.
Against invaders, bacterial infections and infertility.

For jailers and jurors and Jackson, Mississippi.

For kings, Kentucky and Kalamazoo.
Against losing keys.

Against lightning.
For librarians and lawyers.

For mechanics and musicians and mail.
Against mice and mad dogs.

Against fear of night.
For New Orleans and news dealers.

For obsessions and old maids and Ohio.
Against oversleeping.

For plumbers and pawnbrokers and parents of large families.
Against poverty.

For queens and quartermasters.

Against riots and rats.
For rain and against rain.

For silence.

For bomb technicians and medical technicians and television writers.
For reformed thieves and test takers.
Against twitching.

For ugly people and uncontrolled gambling.

For victims of apoplexy, betrayal, child abuse, drowning, incest, jealousy, kidnapping, rape, spouse abuse, stroke, torture, and unfaithfulness.
Against vertigo.

For working people and West Virginia.
Against bad weather.

For expectant mothers, expeditious solutions and excluded people.
Against explosions.

For New York and young people in general.

And one for each tiger crouched in the zoo, stared at by children with no one to pray to and nothing to do.

A Key to Pronunciation: /sälm/

Truly, thou unlockest the spoken word
so that nothing I imagined to say
might be restrained from this rough tongue

snaking up from my peasant heart.
Yea, though I talk through the valley
of the Great Vowel Shift, I fear no

suprasegmentals. Thy virgules
and thy stress marks, they comfort me.
Though I've always licked words

the wrong way and left teeth marks
in their too-soft flesh, thou art patient.
Thou leadest me safely past the landmine

at the beginning of psalm. Thou
makest me a table in the presence
of diphthongs and diacritics. Thou

greaseth my tongue with lateral
approximants and trills. Surely,
eloquence and clarity shall follow me

all the days of my life, and hard words
will dwell tenderly in this mouth forever.

Spurious Entry

*"Ghost words" are usually the product of misreadings or of printers'
errors in previous editions of the dictionary, or simply misbegotten
words that have otherwise achieved some spurious existence.*

I am the ghost word of my father
   in my mother's life. In the mirror, I
see my illegitimate sisters and brothers:

suffarraneous (from *sub* and *grain*) means
   a servant who gets his crumbs from the
chief servant who takes his portion from his master's;

from *gest-rope*, I twist *geist-rope*, a braid of spirits
   for my tail; and make *sangrail*—both the Grail
and pages torn from the book about it—

my bed, my sanguine nest. Though
   the etymology of the verb is uncertain,
not one of the entries for *rape* is spurious.

My mother dropped the charges.

Dear Reader

You have forgotten it all.
You have forgotten your name,
where you lived, who you
loved, why.
        I am simply
your nurse, terse and unlovely.
I point to things
and remind you what they are:
chair, book, daughter, soup.

And when we are alone
I tell you what lies
in each direction: This way
is death, and this way, after
a longer walk, is death,
and that way is death but you
won't see it
until it is right
in front of you.

        Once after
your niece had been to visit you
and I said something about
how you must love her
or she must love you
or something useless like that,
you gripped my forearm
in your terrible swift hand
and said, *she is*

everything—you gave
me a shake—*everything*
to me.

       And then you fell
back into the well. Deep
in the well of everything. And I
stand at the edge and call:

           chair, book, daughter, soup.

Waiting for Lightning

Who I am begins here:
just outside the open door,
my aunt vanishing—

her thick hair a black
nimbus over features
fading in the sunlight,

legs gone in the tangle
of dogs leaping
around her feet, face

translucent as vodka.
I was four and craved
what she was beyond

enduring—the light
inside of her breaking.

THE ALPHABET CONSPIRACY

The word is the making of the world.—Wallace Stevens

It's a filmstrip afternoon
      and we're all grateful
   to the humming projector
      in the middle of our desks,
the closed blinds, the absence of a real adult.

There's a vague promise of revelation
      from the title
   and the dark, tree-lined streets, the voice
      calling from a house
carrying within it our freedom not to answer.

Inside another house, a little girl in a pretty dress
      is falling asleep
   at her father's desk, turning into
      Alice in Wonderland
as her mind falls down the rabbit holes of grammar.

The Mad Hatter and Jabberwocky
      tell her to lure
   the letters into a trap so they can beat them
      to death with mallets.
We'd like to see that. Without words

no one could tell us what to do.
      We know grammar is just a byproduct,
   like schizophrenia, of a brain that grew
      too fast for its own good
and that history is a series of conspiracies

by accidental despots. Mrs. Bradford is
        falling asleep on the wide window ledge,
    her blue polyester pants gapped
        to reveal her white socks
and pink spotted shins. We try not to look.

The Mad Hatter doesn't say that the alphabet
        was first used to keep track of property
    or that for centuries people believed
        if women learned to write
the lost world would never be recovered

or that the Mayans believed
        outsiders wrote things down
    not in order to remember them
        but to free themselves
into the work of forgetting.

That year Mrs. Bradford taught us about
        the Lewis & Clark expedition
    over and over again. We never learned
        why it mattered so much to her
or what possible use it could be to anyone.

The professor tells Judy about
        the thousands of words
   Arabs needed for camels and their parts,
        the dozen words Eskimos had for snow,
and a chimp who learned seven human words.

A voice made visible says:
magic is a matter of fact to you.
Every miracle has to have its qualifications,
reservations, footnotes
and our heads rise from our desks.

The rest of the year will be a series of
substitute teachers
who teach us nothing but footnotes
and their own reservations.
Mrs. Bradford dead of a brain tumor.

We sit in our sixth-grade desks with the blinds
closed against the tree-lined streets
as the letters of the world rise up
and, forming a single word,
eclipse our world and fill our mouths with shadows.

WHO WILL GIVE MY FATHER A NEEDLE, A MOUSE, A CAT, A BIRD?

from a verbal test to determine differences in regional pronunciation

I will. I will give him this needle,
slipped from its red plastic disk,
its tiny eye waiting. He will give me
dark thread which I'll unspool

like the thinnest shadow. I will
give my father a mouse, cut neatly
from the bright illustrated pages
she sleepwalks through. I will give

my father the mouse whose nest
is wrecked, the mouse holding
its own tail in perfect anxiety,
the mouse with its four blind newborns

—tiny naked thumbs—sleeping
fatherless in my house.
I will give my father a cat
for the mice to toy with.

I will give him this bird trapped in a doorway,
a feathered heart with pulsing eyes.
He will give me these hands, my perfect empty nests.

MEANING *TO MILK*

From the Sanskrit *duh*,
        the world gets a stream
of daughters, daughters
        begetting daughters.
From hungry newborns
        opening our mouths
to the sincere milk
        of words, to Jael
with milk and spike for
        the fleeing Canaanite
(whose voice made the walls
        shake and wild animals
fall dead), to young maids
        pulling and pulling
the white streams into
        the pails of morning

HUNGER

is German, its beginning
   soft and sweet as honey,
its ending a growl in the throat

of the wolf who knows your name.
   In other languages,
they *have* hunger, a possession

like an empty suitcase carried
   to the train station. At this stop,
it is *hambre*, like a man

you will dance with; in Lille, *faim*,
   like a woman who listens
to your troubles. In this village,

hunger is *njaa*, an injury
   you don't recover from. Everywhere
it is the dead *nachtigall*

riding on your shoulder,
   the bird who wouldn't eat
though you fed it every morning

while you listened to the radio
   talk about a war
you scarcely believed

was real. It is the seed
in his stomach
turning to stone.

VIVIAN BUCK, 1924 – 1932

. . . [t]hree generations of imbeciles is enough.—Oliver Wendell Holmes Jr.,
in the Supreme Court decision upholding compulsory sterilization

So much can go wrong but, inside,
nothing did. The cells divided,
the ectoderm formed the neural plate,
a crease appeared and deepened,

the folds arched and fused into
the neural tube. Primitive daughter cells
migrated to form a sort of rope ladder
along which neuroblasts traveled.

Your mother knew nothing of this.
In a few hours, while she cleaned
Mrs. Dobbs's kitchen, a heartbeat formed.
Arm buds and leg buds appeared.

The memory of the Dobbs's nephew
faded, his smell and her silence,
as elbows formed and teeth
stationed themselves under your gums.

She was seventeen and believed
she would live in that house
for the rest of her life. You began
to move, your eyelids fused shut

as your irises built themselves
with ligaments, crypts

and furrows. She began to know
what she could not say.

When you were able to
walk and talk and follow directions,
she was sterilized
and released from the Colony

and sent to work for a family
two hundred miles away.
You were good every day. Without knowing
all of the rules, you followed them.

You called them Mr. and Mrs. Dobbs
and cleaned and cooked
and read your books, still
keeping yourself a secret.

You never learned the meaning of enough.

My Mother Crochets the Lord's Last Supper

My sister and I sit at our mother's feet,
studiously watercoloring designs
on her bare legs. My sister paints a map
with a tiny cartouche just above our mother's
thin ankle. A sea monster lurks in the aquamarine,
racing toward my mother's shin. A ship sails,
unaware, behind her knee. We seem invisible
to our mother, two girls bored with summer.

Her eyes focus on her hands that move the needle
drawing up thick white thread from the large spool
beside us. Her mouth moves as if she mumbles a prayer
or a curse under her breath, but she's just keeping count
of the stitches. I paint hunters, my mother's flesh
a cave wall—outlines of human figures shooting
arrows that arc toward running deer, awkward buffalo.

Occasionally she discovers a mistake and unravels
a large section, discarding a half hour's work without pause.

Bondmaid

Of the 414,825 words defined in the first edition of the Oxford English Dictionary,
"bondmaid" was the only one lost. Found long after the fascicle Battentlie-Bozzom
was published, it appeared in a supplement which came out in 1933.

I.

Why do I picture you as blind?
Like Nydia,
the blind flower girl of Pompeii,

who ran through the streets
cupping
her ear. Are you listening for some

sound from the scraps of paper,
the other dark
cubbyholes? Surely there are others

like you, others who would flee.
Illiterate lamb,
who defined you? How many times

and in how many ways have you
been defined?
Here seven abridged quotations put a slave girl in context.

II.

The ancient priests of the tribe of Levi say:
Yf thou wylt haue
bonde seruauntes and maydens

[*thou shalt buy them of the heathen around you*].
In the King James
this is not conditional—you *will* buy them.

[*And whosoever lieth carnally*
with a woman,
that is a bondmaid, betrothed to an husband,

and not at all redeemed, nor freedom given her; she shall
be scourged;
they shall not be put to death, because she was not free.]

III.

The two Scots don't say much, silenced by Shakespeare
and his large vocabulary.
Another man, Spenser, recites a tale of two brothers,

one who was *rauisht of his owne bondmaide.*
The bondmaid's name,
you learn, is Ixione, and you want to learn more about a woman slave

who ravishes instead of being the feast. He says
many words but doesn't
tell you enough. The former prophets of the First Book of Kings

contribute these words to your delineation:
[*Their children that were left*
after them in the land, whom the children of Israel

also were not able utterly to destroy, upon those did Solomon levy]
a tribute of bondservice
[*unto this day*]. And you think, this is the whole

of the bondmaid's role in books of kings.
You do not ask:
but aren't kings mere actors in the great book of slaves?

IV.

And last, never sleeping, is Paul, sick and always writing letters, this one
to the Galatians,
reminding them and you of the story of Hagar: *For it is written,*

that Abraham had two sons, the one by a bondmaid, the other
by a freewoman.
He whispers the rest to you:

But he who was of the bondwoman was born
after the flesh;
but he of the freewoman was by promise. With his hot breath

near, he lists for you the manifest works of the flesh:
adultery, fornication,
uncleanness, lasciviousness, idolatry, witchcraft, hatred, variance,

—the words are piling up, wrapping around you like wet wool—
emulations, wrath, strife,
seditions, heresies—his breath catches, you can feel the spittle

as he draws near—*envyings, murders, drunkenness, revelings.*
And then silence.
Has the man run out of words? He draws back,

you can breathe for a moment; he turns his face
to the wall,
still muttering. You would like to sleep. Is every escape temporary?

V.

The apostle has said that in Christ there is neither male nor female,
neither bond
nor free. Your whole identity erased—imagine!

Is it faith you listen for? How many of us would need to believe
for it to be true?
Our marble legs ache, frozen at the master's gate.

ON THE MAIDEN VOYAGE OF FRANCIS MARION, REVOLUTIONARY WAR HERO

The dog launched his body from the sinking ship,
landing with a splash just a few yards away,
and the six men in the open boat cheered as he swam

to them. They saw him as a lucky omen. And
what else? Unlike the men, he did not think
about shore or anticipate need. He was no prophet.

When Lykanos served human flesh to a god,
some say he was turned into a wolf. Some say the world
was flooded. In the boat, the sailors believed both.

When hunger came like a pale rumor the dog tried
to turn a deaf ear, but the air churned with it—
there was nothing else to breathe. The men swore

at the water, the heat, the cold, the dog and then
stopped talking. On the third night, the mate
—who had not been well—died. The first to notice

was the dog. He licked the hand, cold as night.
It was good. He moved to the sunburnt calf
and sank his teeth in, gently. Despite the roar

in his head the first bite caused, he ate delicately.
But he could not stop the growl that blossomed
in his throat, all gratitude for the Master who provides.

THIS IS THE FINAL DAY AFTER YEARS OF SWEETNESS

The poet's skull is absent
from this pink marble tomb,
replaced with my head.
His right hand too is missing,
stolen by a drunken friar
ages ago. Alive, my right hand
cupped eggs still warm
from the hen, a newborn's head
without ever saying *this is what waits*.
I used every part of me,
every bone pushed against the world
and the world pushed back.
It's the pressure I'll miss
and remember—the tip of his spine
firm as a finger held to my lips.

LILITH VS. THE MOVIE MONSTERS

After school, I assembled the plastic parts of the Wolfman,
gave him a stand to anchor him outside of my dreams
and painted his jacket and lips red,
his teeth a thrill of white—clenched against my name.

Next, I assembled myself from the dead
each part with its own will, barely under my control.
I grunted ones and zeros through the village and feared fire.

In the poetry section of the public library,
I found a cross—ornate and cheap—resting
by the window with a few emaciated volumes. I slept

with it clutched in my right hand, my arms crossed
over my chest against the shadows in my bedroom,
my long white neck exposed to
his long sharp teeth
while the cape descended over and over.

Saint Rita

I went to bed as Gilda
and woke up me again,
still the patron saint
of bad marriages
and atomic bombs
in peace time, still dancing
in black and white.

There are cows dying
of old age in the pasture
and calves with faces of young boys,
steady and self-contained
living out awed lives
in fields of green sway.
They never think of me

and for this I bless them.

THE WHORE'S GUIDE TO ETYMOLOGY

In early brothels, we
used water clocks, small bowls with a hole
        in the bottom placed inside larger
ones. When the small bowl sank we knew

      the man's time was up.
In the Middle Ages, we loved passion plays,
        loved standing in the town square
listening to Herod call our Lord a *brothel*.

      Then it meant a worthless, abandoned fellow;
a good-for-nothing abandoned woman; or a prostitute
        (good for one thing, at least).
The word comes from the combination of *broth* and *el*:

      broth from the Old English
means a liquid in which anything has been boiled,
        (also, obscurely, the essence of a boy);
and *el* means god, like Baal, the one who required

      a sacrifice of our firstborn sons,
like Yahweh who demanded Sarah's boy
        from Abraham but relented
and then arranged the death of his own.

      Again and again, he comes to us
broken by his own hands; he uses our mouths
        to say he's sorry.
And we forgive him.

Ossuary of James

Sitting in the parking lot of the funeral home,
 I picture words of Christ
in red: *Let the dead*

bury the dead. That's easy for him to say,
 rising as he did
after just three days while the rest of us will have to wait

for Judgment Day, wait for Kingdom Come, for him
 to return,
& this time with something more than parables

& a fragile human body that brings out
 the worst in us.
Inside the funeral home, my half-brother James.

The New Testament tells us that Jesus had a brother
 (or half-brother) named
James who wanted nothing to do with miracles.

But after the crucifixion, James refused to eat until
 Jesus appeared & said, "My brother,
eat thy bread, for the son of Man is risen from the dead."

And then James followed faith to his death. Some say
 he was sentenced
by a wicked judge to be stoned, others say he was pushed

from the pinnacle of the Second Temple & then beaten
      with a blacksmith's hammer.
What I know for certain about my own half-brother:

we share the same father, he didn't know
      he had a sister,
he was acquitted in the beating death of an old man

two days before he died alone,
      at the age of 19,
on a rooftop. His good deeds, whatever

they might have been, have gone unrecorded.
      That night, trying
to break into a law office, he got tangled

in his own ropes; with his arms snared above his head,
      his breath like a bone
stuck in his throat until he choked to death.

Exhaustion asphyxia—
      the same cause of death
for criminals & enemies of the state, dying

in agony four & five deep around the city walls.
      When the apostles told Jesus
his family waited outside the temple, he refused them,

saying: *My mother and my brothers—they are those*
       who hear the word of God
and act upon it. I won't go inside. I didn't come to pay

my respects. I don't know why I'm here.
       Watching the mourners,
I test myself to see if I will recognize

my father, our father, whom I've never seen.
       My mother says
I look like him—same eyes, same cheekbones. In

Tel Aviv, a man has been forging biblical artifacts,
       like the Ossuary of James,
changing history, they say, in front of our eyes.

This man had a number of bone boxes, including
       one inscribed "James, son of Joseph";
he simply added "brother of Jesus." James preached:

He who disparages a brother or passes judgment
       on his brother
disparages the law. I have spent my life loving the law

& judging my father, my brother, myself.
       None of the faces
disappearing into the cars looks like mine.

I won't follow the line of cars to the grave.
      I don't want to know
where his bones lie.

Civic Duty

Think of a small Greek fishing village on the eastern coast
of Florida, the streetlights coming on, the streets empty
except for three drunks and a possum.

Beneath a red light, one man pokes a long pole at the animal.
The possum—with fur like aggressive carpet
and a hideous naked tail—lunges and hisses.

Listen to the boats rocking in the harbor, to the hollow,
somber rattle of the masts. Listen to the men's laughter.

THE SIN-EATER

one hired to take upon himself the sins of a deceased
person by means of food eaten above the dead body

That first girl's name has long been forgotten
by everyone save me. She was young, fourteen or so,
and the daughter of a laborer. Then a carriage accident.
How shall I describe it? Her sins smacked of turnips and leeks.

How would innocence taste, I wonder. Pride is like
molded bread, abandoned cake, crumbs in a wood
that all the animals—even the birds—have fled. Save one.
Idolatry mushrooms in the mouth, adultery is a raw onion,

and hatred cooked cabbage—it is what I eat most often.
How do the living not gag on the smell? Will there be another
after me? I am old and full of ghosts. No one speaks to me
without there's been a death. But who needs words?

Most are lies anyway, tasting of pottage. People die,
you can count on them for it, God bless them.
Then over their bodies it's bread and porridge
I eat with clean fingers. I used to follow him,

the old sin-eater, asking him questions:
Was it always the same meal? Did it ever spill?
How much did he eat? Then one day he didn't answer my knock;
inside I found a fresh loaf of bread—three slices cut off—

and a bowl of gruel and him more silent than ever,
under a meal that was venial, mortal, and rotten.

THE OPPOSITE OF FALLING STARS, 1978

My family lives beside the trestle. We
sleep inside the smell of creosote and
beneath the sound of trains rattling:
coal carried to the tipple across the black

Kanawha. I dream wrecks in green valleys;
my sisters dream boys hopping trains; our mother
sleeps in her narrow bed. The coal falls
from its gondolas and the quivering,

bear-brown timber. Days in the alley,
I collect the black chunks and recite
graphite, anthracite, bituminous, lignite.

Staying Under

In the shallow end   of the public swimming pool,
I stood unseen behind my two older sisters,
my head just above water.   They counted to three and
we all went under. My eyes closed against the chlorine
I pictured the sun   on its surface, their faces
when I won. When I reached out to see if they were there
    my hands touched nothing. Then with both hands
        I held my breath down
until I couldn't feel   it matter.

My mother remembers the lifeguard bulleting into the pool
    & how her body felt like the gun that fired him, hard and still.
She remembers a blue daughter coming out of the water,
    CPR & vomiting. My sisters remember a girl dumb enough
to drown herself in three feet of water. I remember becoming
    the blue between sky and water.

Monongah, 1907

In the worst mining accident in U.S. history, the coal company hid the
truth by reducing the number killed by nearly 200 men and boys.

Goods were thrown from the shelves
of the company store,
the river reached for
the railroad tracks, the hill

lunged away from itself.
The houses on the hill
lifted and shook. The bank,
not yet finished,

trembled but its beams held.
Later, the newspapers
printed rumors of incredible
escapes: men shot

straight through air holes,
whole as ever,
and twice as alive. Children
gathered around

the entrances. Women tore
at their hair
and scratched their faces.
The dead were taken

out as they had gone in,
in twos and threes,

and carried to the bank like
something still valuable

and, like something once valuable,
they disappeared
as the counting began.

SEED STORE SESTINA

You can't buy seeds in Matewan, West Virginia, not even at the Seed
Store, the two-story wooden building that stands two blocks from the Tug
River, which swells almost annually into the store, into all of Matewan.
The little town of miners was used to the floods, water black with coal
waste surging into their homes like Baldwin-Felts detectives. Living on the few dollars
the Stone Mountain Coal Company was willing to part with, lungs shot

but nerves and hands always steady with a shot-
gun, the stubborn immigrants waited between the mountains and the river, hayseeds
of the New World. Now, those few who remain have a fifty-million-dollar
wall standing between their six-block town and the river that got its name from tugs
—the shoe leather soldiers once boiled for food. Those steep bare mountains were full of coal
and mothered a boom town until machines came and ate up most of the jobs in Matewan.

Now, you can find optimism discounted at every store here in Matewan,
in both the cafes, and in the barbershop. The floodwall is a good sign, a shot
in the arm, the Nenni Department Store owner tells me. "The coal
money is gone and ain't coming back." Everything has gone to seed,
he knows. He tells me about the new annual arts festival as we watch a dirty white dog tug
at her leash, squat beside the Great Wall—she's unconcerned with tourist dollars.

Mr. Nenni gazes beyond the dog to the wall. "A million-dollar
investment," he muses, "and a real vote of confidence in Matewan."
I drift away as he starts talking about the bass fishing over in the Tug.
I browse, lingering over faded socks and '70s tennis shoes, and finally settle on a shot
glass that reads "The Hatfields & McCoys." I walk down to the Seed
Store, find a note, *I'm at home*, on the open door. Inside are little miner statues made of coal,

some funeral wreaths. An outdoor loudspeaker recounts the showdown of the coal
mine wars. I listen from inside the Seed Store where I spend five dollars
on an amaryllis after the bent-over store owner returns. Plastic jars of seeds,
not for sale, line the counter. Maybe they're magic, intended only for the citizens of Matewan.
Flowery crosses are lined up like starving soldiers beseeching God. I get a shot
of Mrs. Schwartz standing in front of them, holding my amaryllis, a frown tugging

at her mouth. In 1882, Devil Anse Hatfield, his heart an airless chamber, crossed the Tug
Bridge. He knew the timber was dwindling, and they hadn't yet discovered coal.
Pressures were mounting. He executed three McCoys after they'd stabbed and shot
Ellison Hatfield. It's part of the image of violence they now sell for tourist dollars.
The whole state is drunk on the moonshine dream of tourism. Matewan's
been knocking it back one shot at a time; this is how they water their seeds.

Almanac

The Lord God's favorite question
was *where*, as in "where are you"
to Adam, Eve, Moses, et al, like a man
blind as love, or just lonesome;

and we called out "here I am,"
dragging our leaky bags of flesh
over the fields, like wet fingertips
across Braille.

We asked *why* and skirted the holes
of *who*—those shadowy wells our
selves are poured out of, or into. True,
sometimes we fell.

You, diligent almanac, try
to answer *when* and *what* (hardly burning
questions). Poor little fortune teller,
you borrowed red letter days from the church

and your name from Gypsies.
Welcome guest of the farmer and his daughter,
you provide a daily diet of the small answers—
proverbs, astrology, weather, and recipes.

These days, farmers are dying out;
it's been downhill since Cain sacrificed
the first flush of his field (then God's disfavor,
Abel's body, God demanding *where is he*).

Still, you keep reminding us:
*An empty bag cannot stand
upright. He that lives upon hope
will die fasting* no matter where or why.

Whatever You Do

Almost everywhere today the sun and its rays are merciless,
beating down on houses, shouting up from the pavement,

consummating all of our dark ideas. The heat immobilizes a woman
driving to the grocery, leaving her staring senselessly at a green light,

enraging other drivers who just want to go where they are going—*now*.
Fingers grip everything too tightly or too loosely today, the way the heart

grips every day, tightly panicked like the bears inside the zoo, glaring
hopelessly at the sinkhole that has opened but offers no exit. She turns at the

intersection of Herself and Something Else, down a too-familiar street, past a
Jaguar with a flat tire and a fifty-something man in a blue, wrinkled suit on his

knees beside it; his pale hands are awkward with the tire iron, weaker than the chrome
lug nuts—five stubborn stars. Two boys on bicycles quietly watch the sweating

man. Is it possible everything is melting together? Her thighs and the Blue Ridge
Naugahyde seat are becoming one. The day is a Salvador Dalí soup

or a finger painting by a clumsy child. She runs a red light,
parks next to a guy in a Land Rover daydreaming about

quantum field theory. He smiles as if she's part of an exhibit he approves of.
Right outside the supermarket door Girl Scouts sell cookies and

she walks past them not buying, turns down the first aisle
to buy tamari and tofu, though who wants to eat in this heat –

ubiquitous and unwholesome, rubbing thoughts together in her head, all
vying for dominance, trying to get the tongue and lips to free them into the air.

Who wants to shop for the food sitting sullen on the shelves, shrink-wrapped
Xeroxed examples of genetic engineering. She buys conventional mushrooms and

yellow squash. She wanted organic but had wasted her money at the
zoo, whispering words of comfort to the bears when she was alone with them.

Ur: What Signs & Wonders

Driving down an ugly stretch of road
through dissolute Florida towns, we passed
church marquees with their flat-footed attempts
at levity: *What's missing from C-H__C-H?*

U-R. I read this at first as Ur,
the ancient city southeast of Babylon,
ten miles from the Euphrates, the fickle river
that changed its course and wandered away

from Ur, as Abraham did, leaving
a mound of rubble in a desert that once
was a city in a fertile land. Then we saw
a large, abandoned building with a sign

informing the rushing traffic:
"The Center of Hope is Permanently closed."
In the tombs of Ur some strangers found,
among the gold, tablets made of clay

boasting of the eternal temples of dead kings.
But of course temples are temporary by nature.
In this world, even gods are temporary. So is doubt
and faith. This morning when I walked past a store

sign telling me, "We are close,"
I told myself that the Center of Hope
is Permanently close, and for a few blocks
I didn't believe it and for a few blocks I did.

TERRIBLE HOLY JOY: READING THE NORTON ANTHOLOGY OF POETRY IN BED

We take our poetry lying down
And smuggle old words into our sleep.
As we trudge through Pope to get to Brown
We take our poetry lying down.
We take the old women and the boys that drown
And by morning lose every line but keep
"Their terrible holy joy." We take our poetry lying down,
And smuggle old worlds into our sleep.

WATSON AND THE SHARK

by John Singleton Copley, 1778

Why does the naked Watson
reach for the man
harpooning the shark?

Above him, two men reach
far outside their little boat
but the youth strains past,

closer to the gaping mouth
& human eye of the shark.
A matter of composition,

I suppose. The rope
has draped across his arm
just above the pale invitation

inside his elbow, his throat,
his hard ribs, soft waist and
thick muscled thighs. I think

the young man rowing
in the back, with anguished face,
must love you, careless boy—

as the artist does as he mixes
drops of your blood in the water,
as we all do when we love,

our hands frozen around oars,
knowing your eyes suddenly see
what we've seen all along.

THE AMERICAN ON HIS FIRST HONEYMOON

What we can say has already been said
about each painting in the gallery—
about the quality of light, the way she holds her head.

So we are silent in the subway, silent in bed.
Our bodies too are mute; we fall asleep knowing
what we could say has already been said.

Over toast and coffee and the newspaper thoroughly read
the day unfolds between us. I am too weak to carry
this quality of light, the way she holds her head.

I would vow to leave if love had left
if this were the wedding of two gypsies.
But what should I say? It has been said

the dead would properly bury the dead
and here I am, alive at last and buried
by the quality of light, and the way she holds her head.

Perhaps women, sex, love are all over-rated.
Which of us is the artist and which the light? You see,
the words I might say have been better said—
words concerning the quality of light, the way you hold your head.

First Apartment

Our two cats sunned themselves on the roof.
We kept a plastic rocking horse in the living room.
You bought a rabbit from the flea market. For me, you said.
I bought vegetarian cookbooks.
The rooms were big white boxes we could never fill.
The man downstairs drank and tried to sell me his belongings when I came
home from work.

I still have a picture of you smiling on that horse.
The rabbit chewed shoes and books and left little black pellets everywhere.
I built a cage from plywood and chicken wire and put it in our bedroom.
Why not in the living room with the plastic horse, I wonder now.
And why the plastic horse?

For Western Violence and Brief Sensuality: A Rondeau

Riding up and down Monument Valley, the Searchers are led by John Wayne
a man dragging a hollow past behind his horse over the same
stretch of sand. His outrage, rising up like red sandstone, towers over
him, the ex-Confederate who didn't surrender. His brother
and the coveted wife slain, the homestead burnt, the girls stolen—

the outlaw can't just walk away. We hold hands, watching men inflamed
deciding what is civilized and destroying what isn't. The question
is now the niece. We watch the horses going nowhere, feel their
sweet exhaustion from riding up and down Monument Valley.

My head on your chest, I listen to the horses' hooves. My brain
races ahead, night after night, leading the horses to water, thin
streams in dust. Aren't we the fools, and worse, two women wanting to deliver
some innocent, some prairie damsel, from the savage heart? And neither
of us captives. Your body and mine are short trips really, with beautiful terrain.
Who's to say how long we'll last riding up and down Monument Valley?

In the ER Waiting Room with My Girlfriend

Each fevered chair is filled with a girl
her mouth open, yellow breaths passing
through pale lips. She's hoping for a new doctor,
some dilaudid or vicodin. She looks at
the tv. I watch the girls change
into women with wild hair and hard feet
in worn-out slippers, into a college boy
with a busted ankle and some girl he might fall
in love with, into a woman in a wheelchair burying
her blazing head against the man who strokes her
as if she doesn't burn his hands.

The Burning Barn

When I met your dad he told me a joke—
drunk, standing (barely) in that hot kitchen,
all beard and belly, the fat Abner Snopes.
That house, your daddy, your jailbait cousin,
and your brother (out on bail and on the run)
belonged in some Faulkner story. So did you, but
this Sarty grew up to be lesbian,
tougher and drunker than William. A full minute
your father mimicked going down on a woman,
jabbing his tongue between sharp teeth, wetly vile.
Why didn't I see I could walk away, or run?
Transfixed by the exposed soft butter and piles
of over-cooked food, I waited for the punch line
and watched a fly circle and land, circle and land.

The Signal

Give me the seven days in August when
        the wind stopped blowing.
     The sky a blue bathing cap.
        Our limbs straight, poised above the water.
It isn't as if the radio had died.
        It's more like the song itself fell in and drowned
        when we weren't looking.

        Every time we kissed, the board rose higher,
    the water more cold and blue.
Take the trees that aren't moving, their leaves upturned.
        This means it will rain soon.
Stand still.
        You can see the tops of all the houses from here.

This Is Not True

After the wedding, I follow bride and groom down unfamiliar country roads lined
by corn, back to the bride's home. Her 93-year-old aunt is perched in my passenger seat,

cranberry soup from the reception balanced precariously in the back. The bride is
driving fast. In my bridesmaid gown, I work the pedals in bare feet, listening to

Estelle's thick Peruvian accent. Impulsively, I tell her she's fun which is true, but her
family ignores her sly jokes at the dinner table. She seems to be a thread

gone south, slowly coming loose from their fabric. She glances at me sharply, pulls
her hand up to her cheek, turns her face away. The bride runs a yellow light;

I stop at the red. Estelle begins a new story, one about her sister Patty, their yearly
jaunts everywhere until Patty became too sick, was fading out of her skin, leaving Estelle

kneeling in prayer while she took the double-bypass alone. After surgery, Patty kept her
lips closed against food, so Estelle brought in grapes that she had peeled. It was

May and time to travel, but she held still, cut the tender skin of each grape, slipped it off.
Nurses reported Estelle to the doctor, but she said grapes are very good for digestion, an

old cure in Peru. She looks at me. "This is not true. I do not know anything about cures in
Peru, but I know she will eat grapes, and the doctor believes me." She laughs, then goes

quiet. "We had two more trips after that. Glorious trips." I grip the steering wheel harder,
remembering the marinated fish in the back, trips I haven't taken. Estelle and I are alone,

slipping on our days like wet stones. I can't see the taillights of the bride's car. I am so
tired now. On either side, the fields stretch out like dreams I could be having. Beneath an

underpass, a deer leaps in front of us, just a few feet from the hood of the car, our vault within a vault. I pull to the shoulder, let go of the bride. Estelle and I stare out the

windshield. "Last year, a doctor in Peru tells me grapes are a great cure, for recovery—excellent." She turns a wide smile on me. "I did not lie. I just didn't know it was true,

you see?" At the edge of the cornfield, a doe watches, pulling us gently back to the zeros of our clocks. Our *zeitgeber* waits a full minute, then bounds across the road.

Smite, Smitten

My dictionary lists fourteen entries
for the verb *quit*, enough for a sonnet
on unrequited love. Most are rare, e.g.,
"to use one's hands effectively" or "to let
go (something held)." Whatever else they meant
(to put in quiet, set free, absolve), *quit*,
quite & requite all carried this sentiment:
To pay back, to return the favor. Smit-
ten, I would strike you back, if I
could. Each night in my bed we fuck & fuck.
It doesn't make you mine, or make it right.
But I won't quit. I open my hands & shut
my mouth, my stuttered houses. I'm in your debt
and can't get out. At least, not yet. Not quite.

In the Museum of Us

The little wooden man has his sweet face tilted upward, away from the hundreds of rusted nails and metal shards radiating from his torso, his modest hands resting lightly on narrow hips. You note that the figure belonged to a religious elder who drove the desires of his flock into this wooden body, accessing divine power for their fulfillment. A yoke and chain—barely visible for all of the nails—encircle the figure's neck; his belly is a mirror. I look at his upturned face—the vague smile on his mouth, his eyes little mirrors. Is there a resemblance to the agonized face of Christ, with the three nails of human desire—God's hooks—pinning him to his wooden cross? Later, when I am standing alone in front of a painting, the figure takes my hand and we stare with his silver eyes at the faces on the hill gazing up at the winged horse, the man's red crown, the woman's white dress.

THE PLAGIARIST

Each night in a ruined country,
I spraypaint my name on buildings
and bridges. Big black letters,

sometimes red, make all things mine.
In my bed, I use all of the words
you whispered into my skin. When

I open my mouth, it is us I devour. Know:
I erase nothing but your name. This,
my sweet, makes all things true.

Later—in hell—I'll make sure
I quote you. Now repeat after me:
I'm not the one who wrote this.

Within Five Miles of Home

The National Highway Traffic Safety Administration
            has banned its employees from using the word *accident*
because it gives the idea that accidents are outside of human control,

but I have seen my hands twitch the wheel, the chainsaw jump
            from wood to arm, an icy bridge slip a standing man
straight down twenty feet, cigarettes relight after I've fallen asleep.

Even God acknowledges accidents, commanding
            the Israelites to set aside Six Cities of Refuge where anyone
who accidentally killed another must remain until the death of the high priest.

There is a city of refuge inside of me where I wait.
            I wait for thieves to take everything,
for her to remarry, for our children to grow old without me

while she sends word for my return.

Auto Life Fire

This is a legal policy between you and us.

What shall I do, because trouble comes to me and I am overwhelmed by it.

You are liable only for certain things.

I have many thoughts and they put me in danger.

This policy applies only to loss.

Give me a word.

This entire policy is void if, whether before or after loss, you abandon property for any reason.

I have committed a great fault and I cannot acknowledge it.

The following are not covered under this policy: animals, birds or fish.

Is it possible to repent? Why do you avoid me?

You must assign to us your rights of recovery.

Why are the demons so frightened of you?

Like other contracts, it contains certain duties and responsibilities of both parties.

Give me a word that I may be saved.

This is a non-assessable policy.

Give me a word.

Damage to the falling object itself is not covered.

MISHAP

ends with pursed lips and a puff of air
        but starts with a closed mouth
    and vibrating throat

a humming of our first note of ourselves—
      our objective case:
    feed me, love me, watch me

then the subjective: a narrow column
      of impulse and irreverence
    startled perhaps by the hissing

in the middle of the word's path. See
      the curved aching
    toward the whisper of—him? her?

In most other words, the two—
      placed next to each other—
    fuse, shushing our objections.

But this word is cleaved neatly in half. The second
      half is happiness abbreviated:
    not the beginning

of pleasure and then a wrong turn
      but rather a wrong turn
    into a sudden sweet happiness

that catches in your throat

WOMANLESS

a headword in Webster's Tenth New Collegiate Dictionary
for which there is no entry

Like God, like Adam at first:
Dull, until they brought their looking-glass
Into the strange arena of the Garden
And took turns in front of her.
And then God could feel the fruit
Hitting the ground and rotting
Even as he felt it ripen. It was only

Her mouth, her teeth, which could sever
The awful link. What had He done?
And what about me? When I look in a mirror,
I see the parts of a woman; but if *womanless*
Can include me, then womanless like me too,
For a few months here—not in paradise of course,
But close enough—until you. Then nothing was close

Enough. With you I unearth myself and find
Not some wholesome first being latching names
Onto things nor even his supporting actress,
But a long smooth case for a reptilian heart
And an unapologetic forked tongue
Licking at the disappearing line between
What I won't do and what I will.

A HISTORY OF GLASS

When God closes a door, we break a window.
Sorry I say to the landlord who replaces it. *Sorry*
I say the next morning to the neighbor who

complains about the noise. An accident. She
waits for more of an explanation. So I
start at the beginning. The history of glass is a history

of accidents. Long ago and far away: a woman, a pot, a fire.
Her lover surprises her from behind, kisses her
until the pot glows, smoke rising like a choir.

She snatches it from the hearth
& drops it on the floor covered in sand
& ash. (She is a good cook but not tidy.) Her lover

throws water on the whole mess: the sand hisses, her hand
burns. She can hardly see the hard new miracle
forming for the tears in her eyes, at her feet a new obsidian

spreads, clear & eddied. It will be 2000 years until
a tradesman molds by hand the small green & blue
glass animals (housed today on the second floor of a local

museum), & nearly 4000 before sheet glass in 1902.
(Many accidents happen during this period.) One hundred years
later the glass animals in the museum are visited by two

women: one marvels at their wholeness, except for an ear
or a nose or a paw; one does not marvel. She says, "They
survived because they're small." They stop for dinner,

mostly wine. They stumble home. Were there
eyewitnesses at that late hour when they embraced & fell?
Once inside there is a window of sheet glass & a bare

bulb burning out. In the darkness of the stairwell
they sink, dark coats spreading around them. The wind
rushes in. Remember the glass animals? They tell

a history of accidents too—accidents waiting to happen.

You Bring Out the Dead in Me

Not the living dead but the dead dead: the righteous dead
who have waited for the pale horse so they can stop being
so dead. You call forth the callused fingers of Johnny Cash
softened during June-less weeks to my deadened
surface. Everywhere, my skin is whirlpools of fingertips
regaining sensation, waiting. You bring out all of the
dead white men in me—entire anthologies of them, my spine
cracking like a loose canon. Whitman & multitudes of dead
or dying soldiers, Keats & Fanny, Hopkins & God all crowd
up inside me, electric wires writhing. You rewind me to
the moment the dead first began to outnumber the living, when
Lazarus returned to tip the scales back, to stave off the inevitable.
In the invisible cities of the dead, I walk star-lined streets,
multiplied beyond endurance. You have resurrected the
Rita Hayworth in me, the Mae West. And we all rise up, as good as dead.

Notes for Selected Poems

"Intercession"
This poem is for Barbara Hamby.

"*The Whore's Guide to Etymology*"
The history of the parts of the word *brothel* are accurate but the etymology is an invention of the author.

"Bondmaid"
The bracketed material provides the rest of the quotation not included in the *OED*.

"This Is Not For You"
Zeitgeber is a German word meaning literally "time giver." It is defined by *Merriam Webster's 11th Collegiate Dictionary* as "an environmental agent or event that provides the stimulus setting or resetting of a biological clock of an organism."

"*Watson and the Shark*"
This is a painting by the American artist John Singleton Copley and was commissioned by Brooks Watson, who at the time of the attack was a fourteen-year-old orphan serving on a trading ship. Watson lost the lower half of his right leg but survived and went on to become Lord Mayor of London.

"Auto Life Fire"
This poem is a dialogue between an insurance policy and supplicants in *The Sayings of the Desert Fathers*.

Biographical Note

After changing majors every semester, Rita Mae Reese dropped out of college and went to work for a lesbian press. After working there for nearly seven years, she was inspired by a visiting author to go back to school full-time. She earned a BA in American Studies and an MA in Creative Writing at Florida State University and then an MFA at the University of Wisconsin-Madison. While pursuing her MFA, she worked at the *Dictionary of American Regional English* and immersed herself in the online edition of the *Oxford English Dictionary* where she began to find poetry in etymology. She began writing many of the poems that eventually formed *The Alphabet Conspiracy*.

Rita Mae has received a Rona Jaffe Foundation Writers' Award, a Stegner fellowship, and a "Discovery"/The Nation award. Her work has been nominated for a Pushcart Prize and has appeared in journals and anthologies including *The Normal School*, *Imaginative Writing*, *From Where You Dream*, *Blackbird*, *New England Review*, *The Southern Review*, and *The Nation*.

She lives in Madison, Wisconsin with her family.